THE SURVIVOR SPIRIT

Chapter 1
The Reality

What is fear she asked.
Fear is an emotion felt
when in threat he said.
Why do I feel it
ever so often she asked.
It is the lack of confidence
within you, he said.

- She is her fear

Endless thoughts,
Stomach in knots.
Head spinning,
Palms sweating.
This feeling
is the death of me;
Feels *like a catastrophe.*
The monster isn't
under the bed,
It is in my head.

- Monster in my head

Burn the midnight oil,
to excel in my tests;
wondering if I will *be the best*.
Desires of wanting to be the
quintessential smart woman
realising I'm only
a *six out of ten*.
Will I ever be the best?
Or would I blend in with the rest.

- The Best

Tears from the struggles
soak my skin,
from the *hate I get*
for my *melanin.*
Hurt,
destroyed and
buried in the ground.
Hopefully,
my spirit has been found.

- Melanin

Humans are created by
the higher power.
Birth parents carve out
our sculpture.
Yet why do I *loathe my body*?
My reflection in the mirror
causes agony.
I *forgot* that
I am my own beauty;
because of the
standards of society.

- My body

The *brightest star* out of
the billions of stars,
the one my mom tells
it’s you
guiding us from afar.
As she points at
the prettiest one,
I hope I could *have*
seen more of you,
like how often I wake up
to the shining, yellow sun.

- The brightest star

Bitter- sweet relationships,
it's all lovey-dovey
until it flips.
Love fades, and
life becomes mundane.
Unfortunately,
it was *never the same*.

- Never the same

Petals by petals
gently sink.
The plant continues to
wither and shrink.
Just like that,
life proves its fragility.
Now you see me,
now you don't;
is its reality.

- Reality

Chapter 2
Healing

These incidents create
unpleasant emotions;
like the *tides* in the ocean.
They *keep coming back* to me,
Leaving me
cold and frozen.

- Tides

How will I succeed?
If I keep getting *defeated.*
By *none other than,*
me.

- Defeat

I'm starting to *see the sun.*
But after days progress,
I feel like I'm *back*
to square one.
Trying and recovering
every single day;
Only to realise,
this heart of mine
continues to break.

- Repetition

Some days,
I'm *grinning*
ear to ear.
On others,
I want to
disappear.

- Opposites

I know I will get through this.
I'm *stronger*
than my trauma.
This *negative feelings* of mine
will *not persist.*

- Stronger than my trauma

I'm growing in my cocoon,
just like a blue butterfly,
I'll *transform soon.*
I'll flutter my wings,
and continue to *soar higher*
and higher
into the painted sky.

- Transformation

I am getting out
of this mess.
I start to realise
my *progress.*
Just one step at a time.
Little by
little,
I will shine.

- Growth

I still get t*riggered*
when incidents
remind me of
my trauma.
I'm still coping with
this phenomenon.

- Triggers

My wounds are
plastered.
The pain has
subsided.
I'm living life with
more positivity and
my heart is
as light as
a cotton candy.

- Warrior

With endless cycles,
I am a *new human* now.
I'll carry on with
wearing my crown.
My *healing process*
transformed to hope.
I know I will
continue to cope.

\- New Human

Chapter 3
Hope

Seeds grow into
beautiful, green plants.
Similarly, with hope and willingness,
you will *seek what you want.*

- Seek your wants

New days.
New beginnings.
New adventures.
New recovery.
Same, old hope.
The hope that will guide you
out of your misery.

- Same and old hope

Sunrises are special.
For it shows that
there is light
even after the sun sets.
Likewise, when you
are *surrounded by darkness,*
know that you are able to
reignite the *fire within you.*

- Reignite

If you had to make a choice to
only have *one state of mind forever*,
select hope.

For which it consists of
eager,
willpower,
positivity;
and *with these factors,*
you can cope.

- Only one

Even if it's you
against the world,
the survivor spirit you have
will free
your trapped soul.

- Survivor

It’s okay to cry when you struggle.
For that is human nature.
Don’t be ashamed to
let it all out.
In those tears,
I see how much
you *value*
your energy and
soul.

- Know your worth

The energy you put
out into this world.
The prayers
you scream out loud,
to be heard.
The spirit you have
to keep progressing.
It is in the *littlest* things,
that proves,
you are
a *hopeful being.*

- Littlest things

In the tiniest cracks of the paths,
a *flower blooms* its way out
in search of *light.*

Imagine
you are the flower;
Rise and thrive
amidst your challenges.

- Emerge

If hope had an address,
it would have
multiple homes.
For hope lives
in the deepest of souls.

Seek *within yourself;*
search high and low,
your hope will
never let you go.

- Within us all

With hope,
you fuel your soul.
Hope is such a necessity,
like the blood that flows
throughout the body.

- The necessity

You have *survived*
100 percent of your past issues.
You *will overcome* those
that are making
its way to you.
Breathe and slowly let go,
a *rain of positivity*
will wash away
your sorrows.

- You got this

Just like you,
a pink lotus flower
starts growing
beneath the muddy, dirty water.
It *pushes through obstacles* it faces,
and blooms out to freshness,
becoming *stronger*.

With the *survivor spirit*,
it has become
a part of the beautiful nature.

Likewise, through
healing and hope,
you will continue
to *flourish further,*
just like the
pink lotus flower.

- Lotus flower

Made in the USA
Coppell, TX
03 November 2021

65007287R10020